FRANKLIN D. ROOSEVELT

American Hero

by Dr. Hugh Roome

Content Consultant

Nanci R. Vargus, Ed.D.

Professor Emeritus, University of Indianapolis

Reading Consultant

Jeanne M. Clidas, Ph.D.

Reading Specialist

Children's Press®

An Imprint of Scholastic Inc.

Library of Congress Cataloging-in-Publication Data
Names: Roome, Hugh, author.
Title: Franklin D. Roosevelt: American hero/by Hugh Roome.
Description: New York: Children's Press, an imprint of Scholastic Inc., 2017. | Series: Rookie
biographies | Includes index.
Identifiers: LCCN 2017005026| ISBN 9780531232293 (library binding) |
ISBN 9780531238639 (pbk.)
Subjects: LCSH: Roosevelt, Franklin D. (Franklin Delano), 1882-1945—Juvenile literature. | United
States—Politics and government—1933-1945—Juvenile literature. | Presidents—United States—
Biography—Juvenile literature.
Classification: LCC E807 .R629 2017 | DDC 973.917092 [B]—dc23
LC record available at https://lccn.loc.gov/2017005026

Produced by Spooky Cheetah Press
Design by Judith Christ-Lafond
Poem by Jodie Shepherd

© 2018 by Scholastic Inc.

Printed in Malaysia 108

SCHOLASTIC, CHILDREN'S PRESS, ROOKIE BIOGRAPHIES™, and associated logos are trademarks
and/or registered trademarks of Scholastic Inc., 557 Broadway, New York, NY 10012.

1 2 3 4 5 6 7 8 9 10 R 27 26 25 24 23 22 21 20 19 18

Photographs ©: cover main: FPG/Hulton Archive/Getty Images; cover background: Orhan Cam/
Shutterstock; back cover: Bettmann/Getty Images; 3 background: spawns/iStockphoto; 3 bottom:
The Granger Collection; 4: Bettmann/Getty Images; 6: Margaret Bourke-White/The LIFE Picture
Collection/Getty Images; 8: Corbis Historical/Getty Images; 11: Corbis Historical/Getty Images;
12: FDR Presidential Library & Museum; 15: Everett Collection Historical/Alamy Images; 16-17:
Bettmann/Getty Images; 19 background: Bettmann/Getty Images; 19 bottom right: Bettmann/
Getty Images; 20: Stock Montage/Getty Images; 23: Time Life Pictures/Department of Defense/
Getty Images; 24: George Skadding/The LIFE Picture Collection/Getty Images; 26-27: Encyclopedia
Britannica/Library of Congress; 29: Claver Carroll/Getty Images; 30 background: spawns/
iStockphoto; 31 top: creatOR76/Shutterstock; 31 center top: Bettmann/Getty Images; 31 center
bottom: Corbis Historical/Getty Images; 31 bottom: Bettmann/Getty Images; 32 background:
spawns/iStockphoto.

Maps by Mapping Specialists

Sources:
page 21: https://www.archives.gov/education/lessons/fdr-inaugural

TABLE OF CONTENTS

Roosevelt speaks to supporters in 1938.

Meet
Franklin D. Roosevelt

Franklin D. Roosevelt was a great American hero. After he got sick, Roosevelt could not walk. But that did not stop him from following his dreams.

He was born rich. Yet Roosevelt worked hard to help the poor. And he was president of the United States during the worst war ever.

Franklin Delano Roosevelt was born on January 30, 1882, in Hyde Park, New York. His parents were rich. Franklin had pet dogs and ponies. He loved to swim, fish, and sail boats. Franklin did not go to school. A teacher came to his house (below) to give him lessons.

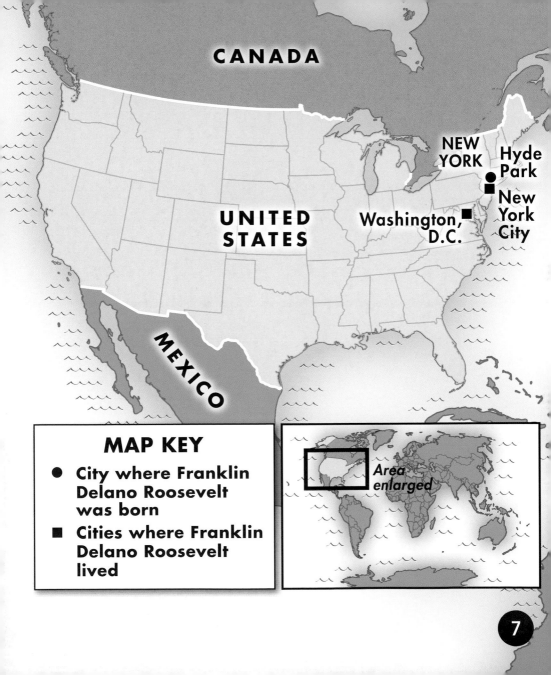

CANADA

NEW
YORK

Hyde
Park

New
York
City

UNITED
STATES

Washington,
D.C.

MEXICO

MAP KEY

- City where Franklin Delano Roosevelt was born
- Cities where Franklin Delano Roosevelt lived

Area enlarged

Eleanor was Franklin's fifth cousin. She was the niece of President Theodore Roosevelt.

When Franklin was a teenager he went to live at a school for rich boys. He was not a great student. Franklin liked sports and played football.

After graduation, Franklin went to Harvard University. He became engaged to Eleanor Roosevelt. They were married in 1905.

When he was 28, Roosevelt was elected to the New York State Senate. He later took a job with the U.S. Navy.

Franklin, Eleanor, and their five children had a great life. Then something terrible happened.

FAST FACT!

The Roosevelt children's names were Anna, James, Elliott, Franklin Jr., and John.

The Roosevelt family

In 1924, Roosevelt spent weeks on his houseboat in Florida. He caught this huge fish! He had hoped the trip would make him feel better.

Roosevelt

Tragedy and Triumph

On August 10, 1921, Roosevelt spent the day boating and swimming with his family. Toward the end of the day, he felt unwell. He went to bed early. When Roosevelt woke up the next morning, he could not move his legs. Doctors said he had a disease called **polio**. He would never walk on his own again.

Roosevelt used steel leg braces and crutches to get around. He worked hard to get better. He was determined to walk again. It was hopeless, though. Roosevelt would never be able to walk—or even stand upright—without help.

FAST FACT!

Roosevelt is known as "FDR."

Roosevelt swam to get strong, but it did not help his legs.

Roosevelt was just at the beginning of his career in **politics** when he got sick. Now he feared he would have to give up his dreams.

FDR had a special car built that he could drive using only his hands—no feet needed.

But Eleanor encouraged her husband to keep fighting.

In 1928, Roosevelt was elected governor of New York.

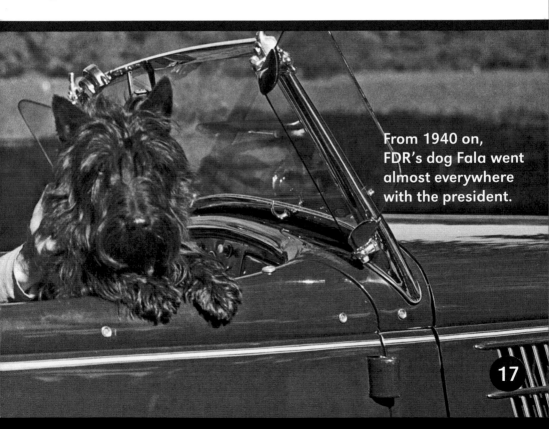

From 1940 on, FDR's dog Fala went almost everywhere with the president.

A New Deal

By the early 1930s, America was in trouble. People could not get jobs. A lot of people lost their homes. Many were hungry. This crisis is known as the **Great Depression**.

Roosevelt said he could fix these problems. In 1932, he ran for president of the United States and won.

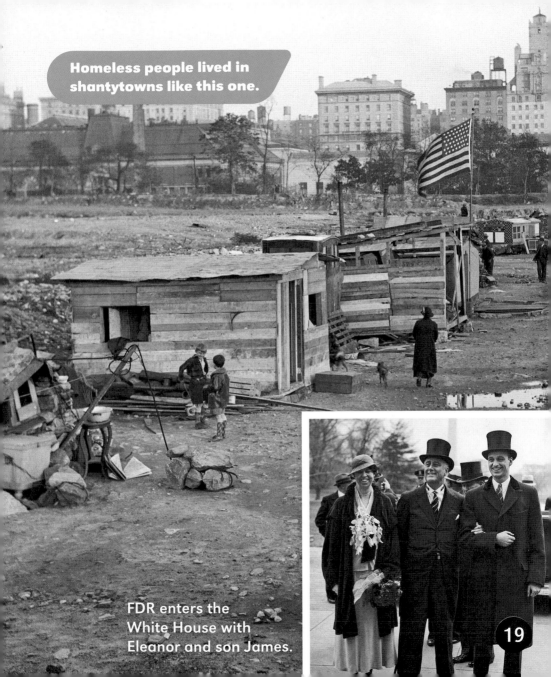

Homeless people lived in shantytowns like this one.

FDR enters the White House with Eleanor and son James.

FDR regularly told the country about his plans. His radio addresses were known as "fireside chats."

FDR spent his first 100 days in office creating programs to help get the American **economy** back on track. He called his plan the New Deal. New Deal programs provided jobs, money, and health care for poor people.

FAST FACT!

FDR told scared Americans, " The only thing we have to fear is fear itself."

The World at War

While Roosevelt was trying to fix America, another terrible thing happened. Two countries got together to try to rule the world. They were Germany and Japan.

Germany used submarines to sink U.S. ships. Japan attacked the U.S. naval base in Hawaii. About 2,400 Americans died.

Nineteen ships were sunk or damaged in the Japanese attack.

23

President Roosevelt gives a speech aboard a naval destroyer.

President Roosevelt

President Roosevelt said the U.S. had to stop these killers. He said Americans would fight until their enemies gave up.

The U.S. fought in World War II from 1941 to 1945. FDR asked everyone to go to work against the enemies. Americans built many more airplanes, warships, and tanks than Japan and Germany did. Brave American soldiers and sailors used them to win the war.

Roosevelt was elected to a fourth term in 1944. But while America grew stronger during the war, FDR grew weaker. He died on April 12, 1945—less than five months before the war finally ended.

FDR meets with the leaders of
Great Britain (left) and Russia
(right) near the end of the war.

27

Franklin D. Roosevelt led the country through the Great Depression and World War II. He dedicated himself to helping people at home and around the world. He is an American hero.

Timeline of Franklin D. Roosevelt's Life

1882 > **1905** > **1910** >

Born on
January 30

Marries Eleanor
on March 17

Elected to
New York
State Senate

...(WHO) SEEK TO ESTABLISH SYSTEMS OF GOVERNMENT BASED ON THE REGIMENTATION OF ALL HUMAN BEINGS BY A HANDFUL OF INDIVIDUAL RULERS... CALL THIS A NEW ORDER. IT IS NOT NEW AND IT IS NOT ORDER.

The FDR Memorial in Washington, D.C., includes a statue of the president's dog Fala.

Elected president for the first of four times

Dies on April 12; World War II ends on September 2

1921 **1932** **1941** **1945**

Stricken with polio

U.S. enters World War II

A Poem About Franklin D. Roosevelt

FDR led the nation for year after year.
Through Depression, in wartime, he never showed fear.
From his struggle with polio, FDR knew
facing problems straight on was the best thing to do.

You Can Be a Leader

 Find a cause you believe in and learn how you can help make a difference.

 Leaders are resilient! Do not let setbacks stop you from working to achieve your goals.

Glossary

- **economy** (i-KAH-nuh-mee): system of buying, selling, making things, and managing money

- **Great Depression** (GRAYT dih-PREH-shun): most serious economic downturn in U.S. history; people lost their jobs, homes, and savings

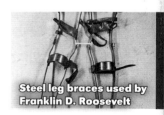

- **polio** (POH-lee-oh): disease that attacks the brain and spinal cord and can cause paralysis

Steel leg braces used by Franklin D. Roosevelt

- **politics** (PAH-luh-tiks): activities, actions, and policies involved in governing a country, state, or city

Index

Facts for Now

Visit this Scholastic Web site for more information on
Franklin D. Roosevelt
and download the Teaching Guide for this series:
www.factsfornow.scholastic.com
Enter the keywords Franklin D. Roosevelt

About the Author

Dr. Hugh Roome is the publisher of Scholastic magazines including
Let's Find Out, *Scholastic News*, and *Storyworks*. He holds a doctorate in
international studies from the Fletcher School, Tufts University. Roome's
father, a World War II naval officer, knew FDR and thought he was America's
greatest president.